Gabriel Dumont

George Woodcock

Fitzhenry & Whiteside

Contents

THE CANADIANS
A Continuing Series

Gabriel Dumont

Author: George Woodcock
Design: Jack Steiner
Cover Illustration: John Mardon

Fitzhenry & Whiteside acknowledge with thanks the Canada Council for the Arts, the Government of Canada through its Book Publishing Industry Development Program, and the Ontario Arts Council for their support of our publishing program.

National Library of Canada Cataloguing in Publication
Woodcock, George, 1912–1995
Gabriel Dumont / George Woodcock.
(Canadians)
Includes index.
ISBN 1-55041-492-5

1. Dumont, Gabriel, 1837-1906. 2. Riel Rebellion, 1885. 3. Métis—Canada, Western—Biography. I. Title. II. Series.
FC3217.1.D84W65 2003   971.05'4'092   C2003-902681-4   F1060.9.D85W66 2003

© 2003 Fitzhenry & Whiteside Limited
195 Allstate Parkway, Markham, Ontario L3R 4T8

Chapter 1
The Dumont Clan and the Métis Nation

If you travel along the South Saskatchewan northward from Saskatoon, you come to a new structure of steel girders and concrete called Gabriel's Bridge. It stands on the site where Gabriel Dumont had his house and ran a ferry over the river. The house was burned by Canadian soldiers during the North West Rebellion of 1885, and now only the name remains to identify the site. A few kilometres north in the little cemetery of Batoche, overlooking the river, a rough boulder marks the site of Dumont's grave. It stands a few metres away from the old wooden church that still bears bullet marks from the historic battle in which Dumont led the Métis in the last days of the North West Rebellion. But there are few other visible signs to evoke the memory of Gabriel Dumont. There are no museum relics of him. He left nothing in writing, except a few documents written by other people to which he added a laboriously drawn cross instead of a signature. For Gabriel Dumont, who spoke all the principal Aboriginal languages of the prairies as well as French, could neither read nor write.

But if Dumont is elusive in terms of tangible relics, his myth is powerful and his place in Canadian history is as secure as that of his people, the Métis. The Métis are the French- and English-speaking people of mixed Aboriginal and European

Gabriel Dumont's grave marker, Batoche cemetery

Annual fur expedition

ancestry, who came into being as fur traders from New France, Scotland and England mingled with the Aboriginal people of the northern forests and, later, of the prairies. The French originally called them *bois-brulés*, people coloured like charred wood. But they themselves have always preferred the name Métis, from the French verb *métisser* —to cross breeds.

The early French traders, called *coureurs de bois*, made their way into the forests west and north of Montreal which they called *le pays d'en haut*— the upper country. In 1696, because of a surplus of furs in the warehouses of Montreal and Quebec, the government of New France revoked the licences under which the *coureurs* operated. Many of them ignored the new regulations and stayed permanently in *le pays d'en haut*, trading in defiance of the law and fathering Métis children. These children inherited their fathers' names, their Catholic religion and a number of European techniques that the Métis added to the wilderness knowledge of their Aboriginal ancestors. As the French fur traders and their Métis sons moved into the prairies, they began to marry Cree women. Eventually they adopted Cree, which was the common trading language west of the Red River, as a second language in addition to their own dialect of French.

As the fur trade developed and spread farther into the North West, the Métis paddled the canoes of the fur brigades, manned the forts scattered on the shores of rivers and lakes and hunted to supply the buffalo meat and pemmican (dried and pounded meat preserved in its own fat) which formed the traders' basic diet. At first it was customary for the traders to return each autumn to their bases in Montreal or on Lake Superior, but eventually they began to winter in the Saskatchewan Valley. In this way the Métis became part of the permanent population of the western plains.

One of the voyageurs who came west to the Saskatchewan in the 1790s and took up employment with the Hudson's Bay Company was a Montreal Frenchman, Jean-Baptiste Dumont. Dumont probably entered the company's service at Edmonton House, established in 1795. Later he served at Fort Carlton and afterwards at Fort Pitt, both on the North Saskatchewan River, and married a pure-blooded Aboriginal of the Sarcee tribe. It was a marriage "according to the custom of the country," which meant that it required only parental consent, since at this time there were no priests west of Red River. The Sarcee were a famous tribe of horsemen and buffalo hunters who lived on the upper reaches of the Athabaska River. Links with this tribe of Aboriginal hunters contributed to the mastery of prairie lore for which Jean-Baptiste's sons and grandsons were celebrated even among the Métis, and to the influence these same men had among the Plains Indians.

Jean-Baptiste, who lived and died in the Saskatchewan Valley, had three sons, Gabriel, Jean and Isidore, and at least one daughter. It was Isidore who became the father of Gabriel Dumont of North West Rebellion fame. Jean-Baptiste's sons grew into tall men "over six feet in height...and heavily built," as the Canadian hunter John Kerr described them. They lived as free hunters. In summer they would kill buffalo and sell the pemmican and hides to the Hudson's Bay Company; in winter they would trap fur-bearing animals and trade with the Aboriginals they met. It was a hard, nomadic life, and the Dumont boys earned the reputation among Hudson's Bay officers of being good trappers and hunters. Among the Aboriginals, they were known as courageous fighters.

Isidore Dumont gained great influence among the Cree, who conferred on him the name Ai-caw-pow, The Stander, to celebrate his reliability. In 1833 when he was 23, Isidore married Louise Laframboise, the daughter of another Métis hunter. Three years later, with his wife and children, Isidore and Pélagie, he hitched up his Red River carts and made the long journey eastward to Red River. The family travelled in the company of Louise Dumont's father and other hunters who formed a convoy for mutual protection against the bands of Sioux who often wandered into the Canadian prairies.

Along the Red River, the Métis had begun to settle in little villages like St. Boniface, St. Vital and Ste Agathe, stretching south from Fort Garry towards the American border. At White Horse Plains, 25 kilometres west on the Assiniboine River, there was a settlement presided over by Cuthbert Grant, the famous Warden of the Plains, who led the great annual buffalo hunts from the Red River into the western prairies. Part French, part Scots and part Aboriginal, Grant regarded himself as the patriarch of the Métis "nation."

The idea of a Métis nation, which was to play so great a part in the Red River rising of 1869 and in the North West Rebellion of 1885, had been alive since the early 1800s. It was first talked of when the North West Company was in bitter dispute with the Hudson's Bay Company and Lord Selkirk over rights of access and hunting in the Red River country. The Northwesters, intent on using the Métis as a private army, encouraged them to think of themselves as a "nation" which, by virtue of its Aboriginal ancestry, had certain rights over the Red River Valley and the western prairies. As a "nation" under their "Captain-General" Cuthbert Grant, the Métis fought against Lord Selkirk's settlers and killed Governor Semple in the skirmish known as the Battle of Seven Oaks near Fort Garry in 1816. The song commemorating that battle, by the hunter bard Pierre Falcon, became a kind of national anthem among the Métis. In the 1830s, when the Métis of the Red River became less nomadic and began to acquire houses at least for winter dwelling, the idea of their aboriginal rights to land in the prairies was revived.

Chapter 2
The World of the Buffalo Hunt

Isidore Dumont settled on one of the long narrow farms beside the Red River at St. Boniface. By the time the Red River census was taken in 1838, he had ploughed one hectare to grow potatoes and barley. His five horses grazed on the rest of his land. He built himself a little mud-plastered house and a barn, and he had a canoe from which he fished on the Red River and Lake Winnipeg. Perhaps most important, he had four Red River carts, made completely of wood. In local terms, this meant prosperity. He could load all four carts with dried meat and pemmican in the buffalo hunting season, and at other times he could earn money carrying freight on the trail that ran along the Red River into American territory at Pembina.

Métis hunters with Red River carts

It was during this unusually settled period in Isidore Dumont's life that his second son, Gabriel, was born in December 1837. By this time, however, Isidore was becoming restless as a riverside farmer. He regretted the loss of the free, roving life of the Saskatchewan, and, in 1839 he gave up his land and went to live with his father-in-law. The next summer, Isidore prepared to return to Fort Pitt, but before he did so he took part in the famous buffalo hunt of 1840.

Each year since he reached the Red River, Isidore Dumont had gone out on the great annual cavalcade in search of the buffalo herds. But the hunt of 1840 was a special occasion, not only because it was the largest that ever went out of Red River, but also because Alexander Ross, one of the best story-tellers of the Old West, accompanied the great hunt and described it in his book, *The Red River Settlement*. In all, 1,630 people gathered for the expedition. Among them were 400 buffalo hunters and 400 children, including Gabriel, aged three, perched under the awning of one of his father's creaking carts. The remaining 800 people were hunters' wives, youths too young to hunt, old men and a few men who were too poor to own horses, but who went to help dry the meat and prepare the pemmican.

Twelve hundred carts formed the core of the cavalcade, screaming on their ungreased wooden axles during the day and forming the defensive rings of the encampment at night. Apart from the horses and oxen that drew the carts, there were 400 select horses belonging to the hunters, which were known as buffalo runners. The whole procession stretched for eight kilometres over the prairie, accompanied by more than 500 dogs. Hundreds of wolves and coyotes followed across the open prairie, hoping to feast on the discarded remnants of the slaughtered beasts.

According to Ross, this unwieldy looking expedition was organized and directed by an efficient and democratic constitution. The hunters from various parts of the Red River Valley gathered, with their carts and horses, at Pembina. There they elected their officers and laid down strict rules. Ten captains of the hunt were chosen, and one was named "the great war chief or head of the camp; and on all public occasions he occupied the place of president." In 1840 the man chosen as chief was a Métis of Scottish and Aboriginal ancestry named Jean-Baptiste Wilkie. Long afterwards, Jean-Baptiste became Gabriel Dumont's father-in-law, and it is just possible that Gabriel actually set eyes on his future wife, Madeleine, during this hunt, for she was born earlier that year at Pembina to Jean-Baptiste and his wife, Isabella Azure.

Before leaving Pembina, Wilkie met with his captains and the other leading hunters, including Isidore Dumont, to vote the rules of the hunt. These were similar to regulations in other hunts—rules making sure that nobody scared the buffalo before the general hunt began; rules establishing the officers' duties; rules providing for punishments which ranged from public shaming to public flogging, after repeated offences. Ross

The World of the Buffalo Hunt

tells us that each of Wilkie's captains had 10 soldiers under his command, and these groups of 10 maintained discipline within the camp in turn, from day to day. There were also 10 rotating guides, each of whom bore the standard of the expedition during his day of office.

Every night of the hunt, the captains and the older hunters would gather to hold their council, "each having his gun, his smoking-bag in his hand, and his pipe in his mouth," to discuss the past day's events and plan for the next day. Ross found their discussion "free, practical and interesting" and remarked on their pride and desire for liberty. "Feeling their own strength, from being constantly armed, and free from control, they despise all others; but above all, they are marvellously tenacious of their own original habits. They cherish freedom as they cherish life."

Such were the Métis at the height of their pride and good fortune, when the buffalo herds seemed endless and formal government was non-existent in the West outside the fur traders' forts. Perhaps the Métis were lawless in that they had no structured government, yet Ross and many other observers agree that the efficiency of the buffalo hunt was achieved through

Shooting a buffalo at close range

rules and restraints that everybody voluntarily accepted and observed. These were the men Gabriel Dumont saw constantly around him when he was a child, the men he admired and imitated and of whom he became one of the last, and perhaps best, examples.

Like all the great buffalo expeditions, the hunt of 1840 was accompanied by its priest. When he had celebrated mass on the morning of departure, the flag was unfurled and the hunt began its journey into the plains at the pace of the oxen-drawn carts. The expedition travelled 19 days before the hunters saw their first herds, dark and dense on the prairie in American territory, somewhere near the Missouri River.

The Métis hunted buffalo by riding through the herd together, shooting from almost point-blank range. It demanded great co-ordination. Everyone must start together; otherwise the herd might stampede too soon and all would be lost. Ross describes the start of the hunt:

> No less than 400 huntsmen, all mounted, and anxiously waiting for the word "Start!" took up their position in a line at one end of the camp, while Captain Wilkie, with his spy-glass at his eye, surveyed the buffalo, examined the ground, and issued his orders. At 8 o'clock the whole cavalcade broke ground, and made for the buffalo; first at a slow trot, then at a gallop, and lastly at full speed.

On that first day 1,375 buffalo were killed. Firing from the hip and loading at the gallop, the best hunters killed 10 or 12 beasts each. By the time the carts arrived, the hunters were already skinning their kills, and when the carcasses reached the camp, the women took over, preparing the pemmican, drying the strips of meat and cleaning the hides.

In mid-August the expedition returned to Red River. Its load of 500 tons of pemmican and dried meat was considered successful, though, as Ross remarked, at least as much usable meat had been left to the wolves. Isidore Dumont sold part of the pemmican and hides that fell to his share to the Hudson's Bay Company in return for goods to trade with the Aboriginals. The rest he kept as provisions for the long journey northwest by the Carlton Trail, back to the Saskatchewan country.

Chapter 3
Initiation into Manhood

The Saskatchewan country was to be the source of Gabriel Dumont's first memories, though in later life he did not recall the journey at cart pace that took him there. Fort Pitt, his childhood home, was, as Paul Kane would see it in 1847, "a neat and compact little fort" of whitewashed buildings within a stockade. A two-pounder gun projected from each of the two stockade turrets. The post was situated between the territories of the Blackfoot and the Cree, so that both these tribes of hereditary enemies traded there. But the abundance of buffalo was so great in this region that fur trading was only a secondary function of Fort Pitt. It operated mainly as a provisioning depot, collecting supplies of pemmican and dried meat to enable traders in other regions, rich in furs but poor in edible game, to survive the winters.

During the winter, Isidore Dumont and his fellow Métis stayed near Fort Pitt in rough log cabins that they built to weather the cold months. At this season game was near to hand, but in the summer they had to go farther afield, travelling as nomads. They loaded all their goods into their Red River carts and camped in the skin tents like those of their Aboriginal kinsmen. They followed the buffalo, netted whitefish and traded on a small scale with the outlying groups of Aboriginals who did not come to the fort.

It was in this semi-nomadic world that Gabriel Dumont grew up. Fort Pitt was the centre of his world; Edmonton House and Fort Carlton were its extremities; and its inhabitants, a mixture of Scottish fur traders, Métis voyageurs and hunters and Aboriginals of many tribes. The Aboriginals treated the Métis as distant relatives and often allowed them to join in their buffalo drives. As a boy Gabriel made many faithful friends among the Cree of his own age. On his father's trading trips he visited his grandmother's people, the Sarcee, and came to

know the Blackfoot and the Gros Ventres, the Assiniboine and the Sioux. He had an extraordinary way with languages; in the end he spoke six Aboriginal languages and French, though he never learned more than a few words of English. Yet he remained illiterate; there was no use for the written word in the world of prairie hunters.

We know very little of what happened to Gabriel and his family between the day in 1840 when they arrived at Fort Pitt and the day in the spring of 1848 when Isidore Dumont decided to join a caravan of hunters returning to Red River. This means that life probably followed a fairly regular routine determined by the seasons—hunting when the chance came, trading with the Aboriginals, feasting and dancing and rest when the hunting and trading were successful. Five other children were born to Isidore and Louise, and six of the eight young Dumonts survived the hazards of infant mortality and the epidemics of smallpox that occasionally swept the prairies.

Gabriel Dumont

Gabriel Dumont did much more than survive. He grew into a strong, stocky boy. Never as tall as his father and uncles, he was squarely built with an immense chest. His face was strong and well shaped, with high Aboriginal cheekbones, the dark sharp eyes of those who habitually look into distances and a wide, rather coarse-lipped mouth. The general impression was of great physical vitality.

There are many kinds of education, not all dependent on reading and writing, and Gabriel's schooling was excellent of its kind, for it turned him into a good hunter and plainsman. At 10 he could ride a pony and break one in. Long before he was given a gun he could shoot with deadly accuracy the bow used by his grandmother's people, the Sarcee. Gabriel also learned from the Sarcee the rare art of calling the buffalo and took part in some of their buffalo slaughters by driving the beasts into pounds or immense traps. He was a good fisherman and canoe-man and, rare among the Métis, an excellent swimmer. He became one of the best Métis guides and, as one of his friends said long afterwards, Gabriel Dumont knew the prairie "as a sheep knows its heath."

We do not know for certain why Isidore Dumont decided to leave the good hunting of Fort Pitt in 1848. It may have been the nomadic instinct that made most of the Métis reluctant to settle in any one place. Or it may have been the news percolating across the prairie that the Red River colony was in a state of unrest because the Métis wanted a share in the trade with the United States, which was monopolized by the Hudson's Bay Company. Certainly Isidore Dumont and his fellow hunters, Alexis Fisher and Petit Cayen, must have talked about these matters as their little cavalcade wandered over the hills and parklands of the Carlton Trail. But for Gabriel, a boy of 10, it was the immediate experiences of the road that were exciting, especially the adventure that led to the presentation of his first gun.

One night near Fort Ellice, the camp was bothered by fierce mosquitoes. Young Isidore and Gabriel were sent to make smudge fires on the windward side of the camp, and as they were gathering dry branches on a nearby bluff, Gabriel heard the sound of many hooves. He thought the camp was about to be attacked by the Sioux, who often raided in this country, and ran to warn his father. He wanted to help in the defence and asked for one of the flintlock muskets the hunters carried. The fires were quickly put out and Isidore Dumont went towards the bluff where he knelt and put his ear to the ground. He stood up with a look of relief. "They are not horsemen! They are buffalo." A short while later the herd came surging out of the darkness and ran by the camp. Afterwards, when the hunters and their families gathered round the relit campfire, they teased Gabriel for his mistake. But his uncle, Alexis Fisher, pointed out that even if the boy could not yet distinguish between the sounds of horse and buffalo hooves, his courage had been amply displayed. When he thought the Sioux were coming, he had not hidden in his mother's lap but had asked for a gun. He should have his gun. Fisher picked a stubby trading musket and gave it to Gabriel, who called it Le Petit, the name he gave to all his favourite rifles. Very soon he became as skilled with his gun as with his bow.

Isidore Dumont did not take up farmland in the Red River villages. Instead, he settled at White Horse Plains, in the open prairie west of Fort Garry, where the inhabitants were mainly nomads living in rough shacks near the Assiniboine who spend most of their time hunting and trading. White Horse Plains became the summer depot of the Dumont family, and from here they joined the annual buffalo hunts into the Missouri country. Each winter they would go to the Qu'Appelle Lakes, where Isidore had built another Métis log cabin. Here he carried on his trade with the local Aboriginals, exchanging knives, hatchets, blankets, ammunition and sometimes a little liquor for buffalo robes, wolf pelts and the occasional fox or beaver skin.

In the summer of 1851 there was a dramatic break in the hunting routine, for the great hunt of that year ended in the famous battle of Grand Coteau, in which the Métis of White Horse Plains defeated the Teton Sioux. That summer 300 people, including 67 hunters and the young Gabriel Dumont, set out from White Horse Plains under the leadership of Baptiste Falcon and accompanied by Father Lafleche, grand vicar to the bishop of St. Boniface. At Pembina they met the hunters from the Red River village but, because of some forgotten disagreement, decided to go their own way and keep in touch with the larger party in case of trouble.

The White Horse Plains party set off in the direction of Devil's Lake in Dakota. After days of uneventful travel, they reached the escarpment that runs up from the Missouri into the Canadian prairies. Known as the Grand Coteau, it is a place of bleak buttes, moraines and wooded coulees. The Coteau was a great refuge for game but also a perfect spot for ambushes. Advancing behind a screen of scouts, the Métis discovered a great encampment of the Sioux—five or six hundred lodges, which meant about 2,500 warriors. The Métis did not know that the Sioux had gathered to put an end to the Red River hunt on land that the Aboriginals regarded as their own. But expecting some kind of attack, the Metis halted immediately and began to turn their train of carts into a fortress.

The 200 carts were drawn into a circle, wheel to wheel. Poles were pushed through the wheels from cart to cart to prevent them from being pulled away from outside. Bedding and bundles of meat and pemmican were stuffed under the carts to strengthen the barricade, within which the animals were herded. The women and children sheltered in shallow trenches. The hunters dug rifle pits to form a circle in the open prairie, about 50 metres outside the barrier of carts.

Meanwhile, the Sioux surrounded a group of five hunters who had gone out to spy. Two of the Métis escaped to give warning, and the 64 remaining hunters and 13 boys who could handle a gun, Gabriel Dumont among them, immediately manned the rifle pits. Isidore hesitated to put his young son, not yet 14, into such danger, but Gabriel insisted and stayed at his post throughout the fight. He lay behind sacks of dried meat, where, as he recounted long afterwards, he was able to "eat the ramparts." The only man who did not take a rifle was Father Lafleche. He remained within the circle of carts to comfort the women and children, but he had an axe beside him so that, if the Aboriginals broke through the circle, he would go down fighting.

Métis family

The circle never was broken. The first day, the Sioux engaged in evasive parleys and tried to catch the Métis off guard. When the Sioux withdrew that night, Baptiste Falcon sent messengers to find the Red River party. During the night his sentries watched with awe under a lunar eclipse. At dawn Father Lafleche celebrated mass. As he ended, the Sioux appeared, decked out for battle and singing war songs. To the Métis they seemed numberless, as the low rays of the sun flashed on their guns and lance tips. After an unsuccessful parley between Chief White Horse and the Métis leaders, the Sioux began to attack in the traditional manner, charging wildly and riding round and round the encampment, firing guns and shooting arrows. In the confusion, two of the captured Métis escaped, but the third was recaptured and killed by the Sioux. The Métis kept up a steady fire from their rifle pits, and within the camp Father Lafleche held his cross high and called on the defenders to have courage.

The battle settled into a stalemate. The Sioux prevented the Métis from moving, but at the cost of exposing themselves to the fire of the well-concealed hunters. Finally, having lost—according to the Métis account—80 men, the Sioux retreated at the end of the day. One of the chiefs cried out, "The Wagon-men have a Manitou with them. That's why we cannot kill them!" He was referring to Father Lafleche. In the minds of the Sioux, the eclipse of the previous night and the sudden thunderstorm that came at the end of the day of fighting were linked to the gestures of the brilliantly robed priest.

The next morning the Métis decided to retreat in the direction of the Red River party. They once again threw out a screen of scouts and this time formed the carts into four columns that could be swung into a defensive position at short notice. They had only been on their way an hour when one of the scouts signalled to them that the Sioux were in pursuit. The carts quickly formed a circle and the defence began again. The Sioux charged and skirmished but to no avail. After five hours, there was another great thunderstorm, during which the Sioux made a last shouting ride around the camp and rode away. Shortly afterwards the Red River hunters arrived, accompanied by 300 Saulteaux, but the Sioux did not return to do battle. Indeed, they never again made a major attack on the Métis.

Chapter 4
Leader of the Hunt

Gabriel Dumont emerged unhurt and excited from his first battle. Still an adolescent, he had endured one of the trials that, in the Métis world, led to the recognition of manhood. He worked hard to perfect his riding skills and his marksmanship, which became so accurate that he could shoot a duck through the head at a hundred paces. He combined the two skills into that perfect combination of timing and aim that was achieved only by the best of the buffalo hunters as they galloped at full speed into the herd.

These years, during which he developed into a famous hunter, were largely shaped by the changing pattern of the western buffalo hunt. As the buffalo diminished in the central prairies, the White Horse Plains hunters began to hunt farther to the northwest. They wintered more often in the regions around Fort Ellice or Qu'Appelle, though the Red River remained their principal trading centre. This meant that they developed closer connections with the Aboriginals of the western plains, in which the Dumonts had a special advantage because of their Sarcee ancestry. Through these links, during his later teens, Gabriel Dumont perfected his unrivalled skills in prairie hunting and fighting and his knowledge of the languages spoken by almost every tribe north of the U.S.–Canadian boundary.

The year 1858 was of special importance in Gabriel Dumont's life. There was a great smallpox epidemic, and Isidore and his family wandered the Saskatchewan Valley to avoid the sickness. There, Gabriel's mother Louise died, not of smallpox, but possibly of tuberculosis, which was already becoming a scourge among the Métis. After his mother's death, Gabriel married Madeleine Wilkie, daughter of Jean-Baptiste Wilkie, chief of many buffalo hunts since 1840 and now a trader at Fort Ellice.

Madeleine, a fresh, capable young woman of 18, was an excellent partner. She often accompanied Gabriel on the hunt, willingly enduring the hard life and work. She did a great deal of the family trading and would sometimes travel down the Carlton Trail to Winnipeg in the company of other Métis to sell the skins and hides Gabriel had collected. Unlike Gabriel, she could speak English, which was an advantage in trading. She had the reputation of being pious, was hospitable to missionaries and was remembered as always ready to help those less fortunate than herself. She and Gabriel were devoted to

Gabriel Dumont

each other and, in Métis terms, their relationship was an unusually companionable one. When an Aboriginal once behaved offensively to Madeleine, Gabriel remarked, "We are always together, and what is done to her is as if it were done to me." They had no children, which was a deep sorrow for both of them. To make up for this emptiness, they adopted a girl called Annie, who was probably related to Madeleine, and in later years Gabriel treated his cousin Jean's child, Alexis Dumont, like a son.

During the years immediately after his marriage, Gabriel continued to hunt in the Saskatchewan country and to trade at the Red River. Soon he began to acquire a reputation not only as a hunter but also as a leader and clever diplomat in relations between the Métis and the Aboriginals, who still shared between them the domination of the prairies. The Métis and the Cree had always lived in relative harmony, but the Sioux remained hostile. Finally in 1862, when the Sioux chiefs felt their tribe threatened by American advances, they decided the time had come for peace. The leading members of the Dumont clan— Gabriel, his father Isidore and his uncle Jean—met the Sioux chiefs at Devil's Lake in Dakota and drew up a peace treaty that neither side broke. A few years later, the Dumonts were responsible for a similar treaty with the Blackfoot.

About the time of the Devil's Lake treaty, Gabriel became the leader of a small group of hunters in the Saskatchewan country who travelled together for mutual protection even when the great hunts were not in progress. Shortly afterwards, with other groups who had been operating in the Touchwood Hills, they moved to the vicinity of Fort Carlton. There were more than 200 hunters, and they decided to create an organization for regulating their hunts, like the one that had existed on the Red River, and to choose a permanent chief. Gabriel was chosen and, at the age of 25, became head of the Saskatchewan hunt. From that time onward, he remained chief of all the Métis who wintered in the region. He assumed leadership at a crucial time in Métis history, when the end of the old nomadic life was already in sight.

Chapter 5
Dumont and the Red River Rising

Paul Kane

In 1848 when Paul Kane went to the Saskatchewan country, he found the buffalo so numerous and so tame that they even wandered into the stockade at Fort Pitt. "They were probably migrating northwards," he suggested, "to escape from the human migrations which are so rapidly filling up the southern and western regions, which were formerly their pasture grounds." Kane's supposition was correct. The abundance of buffalo in the Saskatchewan country corresponded to their decline in the Missouri country, which had been the region of the Red River hunt. For at least a decade after 1848 the hunting around Fort Pitt was still excellent. But by 1862 when Milton and Cheadle travelled through the Saskatchewan country, the herds were dying off. In their book, *The North-West Passage by Land*, these aristocratic English travellers recorded that on the Saskatchewan, "The buffalo have receded so far from the forts, and the quantity of whitefish...has decreased so greatly, that now a winter rarely passes without serious suffering from want of food."

For centuries the Aboriginal methods of hunting had kept the numbers of buffalo stable, but after the introduction of firearms into the prairies, an irreversible decline of the herds began. Men of foresight became concerned for the lives of the plains people when the great herds disappeared. Many missionaries, travellers, Métis leaders and Aboriginal chiefs understood the threat to the prairie dwellers and recognized how important land would one day be. When the buffalo went, only the land would be left, and the Aboriginal peoples must make sure that the land was not lost to them. This was one of the reasons why Catholic missionaries who arrived in the 1860s encouraged the

Métis to settle around their churches. But even earlier, some of the Métis had themselves decided to turn their winter villages of hastily built shacks into more permanent settlements. The first on the South Saskatchewan was founded by the hunters under Gabriel Dumont's leadership. This settlement was called La Petite Ville—the small town—and it stood on the west bank of the Saskatchewan near the present site of Saskatoon. Late in the summer of 1868, a stocky Breton priest named Father André appeared at La Petite Ville. He won the trust of Gabriel Dumont and their friendship was to have important consequences for the Saskatchewan Métis.

Meanwhile, far east on the Red River, the Métis of the riverfront villages began to foresee that distant political events might change their lives. The Confederation of Canada came in 1867. In 1869 the Hudson's Bay Company transferred to the new Dominion the great region known as Rupert's Land between the Shield and the Rocky Mountains, land which they held under a 1660 charter granted by King Charles II. The Red River settlements lay in the centre of this region but they were never consulted about the land transfer. And even before the territory was officially transferred, the Canadian government illegally sent its surveyors to mark out the land.

Having received no legal titles to their river lots, the Métis were disturbed by such arbitrary actions and under the leadership of Louis Riel, they stopped the surveyors and formed a National Committee of the Métis of the Red River. The Committee halted Canadian Lieutenant-Governor McDougall as he tried to cross the border at Pembina; they formed a provisional government under Riel and a militia of mounted Métis organized like the traditional buffalo hunt, with Ambroise Lépine as general.

The news of events on the Red River also disturbed the hunters living on the western plains. Gabriel Dumont was so concerned that he made at least one journey to Fort Garry to confer with Riel and offer his assistance. They met in June 1870, after the agreement between the Canadian government and Riel's provisional government had been completed and the province of Manitoba was being founded. A British–Canadian military expedition under Colonel Wolseley was advancing across the Shield, and it was evident that the military was hostile towards Riel and the other Métis leaders. Dumont advised Riel to begin guerrilla warfare against Wolseley's column with the aid of the Aboriginals of

Lake of the Woods. He offered to bring 500 armed and mounted Métis and Aboriginals, but Riel refused.

Gabriel then went back to the Saskatchewan and spent most of the summer of 1870 travelling between Red River and the Rockies. He wanted to strengthen friendships with the Aboriginals and lay foundations for an alliance of the Aboriginal people to resist further losses of their land and their rights.

Resistance, however, was far from the intention of the priests who were now replacing their roving missions with settled parishes, where the hunters were encouraged to build permanent houses and cultivate the land. In 1871 Father André established the parish of St. Laurent on the west bank of the South Saskatchewan. In 1876 a parish was created at Duck Lake. In 1881 another parish, St. Antoine de Padoue, was founded on the east bank by Father Vegreville. Here, in 1871, a Métis trader named Xavier Letendre had established a store and a ferry, and since his nickname was Batoche, this was the name commonly applied to the village.

The Métis hunters under Gabriel Dumont's leadership left La Petite Ville and the smaller, less permanent settlements of the nomad days, and marked out narrow riverside lots at St. Laurent and Batoche. Gabriel Dumont chose a spot south of Batoche. He realized that the place where the old Hudson's Bay scow used to ferry the Saskatchewan provided a route to Fort Carlton 30 kilometres shorter than that via Batoche's Crossing 10 kilometres down river. Accordingly, he staked out a patch of meadow and woodland running down to the river, started his own ferry in 1872, and in 1873 built a house of logs plastered with clay and whitewash. Later he added a store with a billiard table.

Yet Gabriel Dumont would remain a hunter for the rest of his life, and as long as the annual cavalcade went out from St. Laurent to follow the dwindling buffalo herds, he rode at its head. The last hunt he led was that of 1881; afterwards there were not enough buffalo to be worth hunting.

Ad for ferry service at Gabriel's Crossing

Chapter 6
The Republic of St. Laurent

In 1873 Gabriel Dumont became involved in the first attempts to organize self-government in the western prairies. The structure of the buffalo hunt had survived more or less unchanged since the days of the Red River hunt, but it was only a temporary arrangement lasting about two months every summer, and there was no permanent organization among the groups of Métis scattered over the region during the autumn and winter. As settlements began to form around Batoche and St. Laurent, a permanent population of more than a thousand people clustered together. It seemed clear, at least to Father André, that some kind of local government should be established. Though themselves Frenchmen, the priests sympathized with the Métis' desire to retain their separate identity, and they saw self-governed communities as a way of defending Métis interests.

Gabriel Dumont immediately saw the virtue of Father André's proposal and agreed to call the Métis together to discuss and vote on a local government. On December 10, 1873, the people of the South Saskatchewan settlements gathered in a mass meeting outside the church doors of St. Laurent to create the first government ever established in Canada west of the Red River. Gabriel Dumont presided over the gathering; Father André acted as secretary and the assembled Métis created a constitution for their "community," as they called it. They denied any wish to make themselves independent. Indeed, they stated that "in making their laws, they regard themselves as loyal and faithful subjects of Canada, and are prepared to abandon their own organization and to submit to the laws of the Dominion as soon as Canada establishes regular magistrates with a force sufficient to maintain in the territory the authority of the law."

The old organization of the buffalo hunt provided the basis for the community of St. Laurent. Gabriel Dumont was named president, with a council of eight. Then the assembly enacted

Dumont

the 28 basic laws of the community of St. Laurent. These provided for the councillors to be assisted by an organization of captains and soldiers who would act as the community's police force. The council would meet at least once a month. It would act as a court to judge offences against the laws and to settle differences; it would administer public services and have the power to raise taxes and to require people to work on projects important to the community.

The list of specified crimes gives an interesting insight into this community of hunters and traders. There were penalties for taking other men's horses, for dishonouring women and then refusing to marry them, for lighting fires on the prairie in high summer, for failure to restrain horses that became nuisances or dogs that killed young foals, and for slandering other members of the community. All these crimes were punished by fines; there was no mention of corporal punishment and imprisonment did not figure in the Métis view of a just society. But many crimes familiar to our society were absent from the code of St. Laurent. There was no mention of theft, other than horse theft, perhaps because this crime was extremely rare among the Métis. Nor was there any provision for such violent crimes as assault, manslaughter and murder. Perhaps the assembly felt it wise to leave such matters to existing custom, trusting their laws to reduce the number of excuses for violent acts.

There is no record of the actual meetings of Dumont's council, but since no record of complaints exists, we can assume that its proceedings were carried out with the fairness for which Dumont was celebrated. He himself was so pleased with the experiment that he sent messages to other Métis communities around Qu'Appelle and Edmonton, suggesting they follow suit. He proposed to John McKay, an English-speaking Métis leader in Prince Albert, that they should co-operate in setting up self-government in the North West. Dumont seems to have envisioned a federation of communities that would face the Canadian authorities, when they moved into the prairies, with a network of efficient local governments. Unfortunately, nothing came of his suggestions, and the community of St. Laurent stood in isolation.

Gabriel Dumont and his council were anxious for the people in general to participate in their own government. When a difficult question like that of land rights came up, Gabriel ruled that it was beyond the discretion of the council and called a special general assembly. The assembly met in February 1874, and adapted the land-holding customs of the Québécois on the St. Lawrence to suit the special circumstances of hunters along the South Saskatchewan. Every head of a family should have a strip of land 400 metres wide on the riverfront, running back three kilometres into the prairie. For each son older than 20, an additional plot of the same size could be claimed. Areas useless for cultivating or pasture were regarded as common land, where the entire community could cut wood. The people of St. Laurent, who understood the importance of conservation, denounced "the useless destruction of trees" and decreed that "nobody shall fell more trees than he is capable of using in two weeks." Finally, to resolve any boundary dispute, the council could appoint a commission of three men to visit the land in question and settle the matter.

On December 10, 1874, exactly a year after the establishment of their constitution, the people of St. Laurent gathered again in general assembly, and the president and council surrendered their powers. But after a show of reluctance, Gabriel Dumont agreed to serve again as president, with a slightly different council from that of the previous year. This time the assembly voted no new laws but simply ratified what the council had decreed in the past year.

Dumont and the other leaders now turned to the problem that loomed as large in their minds as land rights: the fate of the buffalo hunt. Even the most optimistic of them could no longer ignore the wasteful slaughter of the herds in the past. And now the buffalo were being attacked by enemies unknown before, sportsmen killing for trophies and professional hunters killing for robes. The St. Laurent hunters had had an especially bad year in 1874, and though most of them blamed the drought that had burned up so much of their hunting grounds, Dumont and the more experienced men were already aware that the buffalo herds were dying.

The new hunt laws that Dumont and the St. Laurent council passed on January 27, 1875 were a compromise between those who believed the buffalo would be there forever and those who knew the great hunts were past. Old rules were strengthened—those forbidding anyone to hunt the buffalo before the leader's signal and those regarding the defensive circle of carts, sentry duty at night and care in making fires. But for the first time there were also laws against wastefulness, and men could be fined for not making full use of buffalo they had killed. It was a measure of conservation too late and too little to make any significant difference to the fate of the buffalo. But it showed an anxiety over the future that had not existed among the Métis when they had killed the great beasts merely for the tender cuts and had left the rest to scavenging wolves. Of all the 25 rules of the buffalo hunt that were passed in January 1875, the most historically significant was Article 23. This declared that any party of Métis in the neighbourhood of the "great caravan," even though they claimed to be independent, should be bound in their hunting by the decisions of the "council of the great camp." Those who did not accept such decisions willingly should be "obliged by force."

So far as we know, the passage of the new hunt laws in January 1875 was the last public act of the president and council of St. Laurent. The following summer a drastic application of Article 23 brought the council's activities to an abrupt end and, for the first time, projected Gabriel Dumont into actual conflict with the Canadian authorities. Winnipeg and Toronto newspapers reported the incident sensationally, and prematurely, as a new Métis rebellion.

The facts are quite simple. When the hunt was assembling at St. Laurent in mid June, it was reported that a group of so-called "free hunters" (in fact operating on behalf of the Hudson's Bay Company) had set off 10 days before. They included French- and English-speaking Métis and Aboriginals. When he heard of this infringement of accepted custom, Gabriel Dumont had a letter written in his name and sent by messenger. It called upon the offending hunters to join the great camp and threatened that if they did not, the *cavaliers* would bring them in and fine them for any *dommage* they had done.

Peter Ballendine, the former Hudson's Bay employee who led the independent expedition, instructed his followers to ignore

Dumont's order, even though some of them were Métis from
St. Laurent who had accepted the council's rules for the buffalo
hunt. Dumont rode in pursuit with 40 of his hunters. When
Ballendine's party refused to go with him, Dumont fined the
Métis who were among them and then impounded goods to
the value of the fines. The Anglophone Métis and the Aboriginals
appear to have been untouched, yet Ballendine carried a com-
plaint to Lawrence Clarke, the Hudson's Bay factor at Fort
Carlton who had recently been appointed justice of the peace
without any police force to support his authority.

Clarke was sensitive to his own powerlessness and jealous
of the authority that Gabriel Dumont exercised in the South
Saskatchewan villages. He believed the incident involving
Dumont and Ballendine provided an excuse for calling
in outside forces and wrote a highly exaggerated
report to the lieutenant-governor of the
Northwest Territories, Alexander Morris.
Clarke reported:

> ...a Court has been constituted numbering fourteen
> persons presided over by a Man named Gabriel
> Dumont who is designated as "President" and
> before whom all delinquents are made to appear,
> or suffer violence in person or property...
>
> This court pretends further to have the power
> to enforce their Laws upon all Indians, Settlers
> and Hunters who frequent the Prairie country in
> the lower section of the Saskatchewan, and have
> levied by violence and Robbery large sums of money of
> inoffensive persons who resort to the Buffalo country for
> a livelihood.

Clarke was encouraged by the Hudson's Bay
Company's chief commissioner, James A. Grahame, who
happened to be in Fort Carlton at the time, and Grahame
delivered the document personally to Lieutenant-Governor
Morris. Morris was aware of Clarke's volatile nature, and he
consulted James McKay, an Anglophone Métis and member of
the Territorial Council, who replied that Dumont and his followers had quite obviously been doing nothing more than
implementing the traditional rules of the hunt. But even with
McKay's advice, Morris could not ignore the precedent of the

Alexander Morris

The Republic of St. Laurent

Major-General E. Selby-Smythe

Red River rising. Therefore, he treated the situation on the South Saskatchewan as potentially dangerous and sent an urgent message to Major-General Sir E. Selby-Smythe, the commander of the Canadian militia, who was travelling the prairies to assess the effectiveness of the new North West Mounted Police. Selby-Smythe and Commissioner French of the mounted police decided to travel to Fort Carlton from Swan River with a force of 50 men—the first mounted police to enter the Saskatchewan country. They would be a "party of observation" that might also help end "the spread of mischievous complications with the half-breeds."

In eight days Selby-Smythe and his party covered the 435 kilometres across the northern parkland to Fort Carlton. With no intention of being used by Clarke, they played their hands very coolly, interviewing Dumont secretly at Gabriel's Crossing before they reached Fort Carlton to face Clarke and witnesses he had gathered. Commissioner French telegraphed to Edward Blake, the minister of justice, that "the outrages by half-breeds in this vicinity are of a trivial nature," and shortly afterwards showed his disapproval of Clarke's action by remarking, "His Honour, and I fear the Dominion Government have been unnecessarily agitated by the alarming reports received."

Selby-Smythe and French departed, leaving Inspector Leif Crozier with a dozen men and instructions to arrest Dumont when he came in from the hunting ground. But Crozier merely discussed the situation with the Métis chief and concluded that Dumont had done nothing wrong according to prairie custom. Later, the Earl of Carnarvon, who was then colonial secretary in the imperial government, ruled that "it would be difficult to take strong exception to the acts of a community which appears to have honestly endeavoured to maintain order by the best means in its power."

Chapter 7
Storm Clouds on the Saskatchewan

The confrontation of 1875 was a sign of great changes soon to come in the Saskatchewan country. In 1875 the mounted police established their district headquarters at Telegraph Flats, the settlement that became Battleford, a little way up the North Saskatchewan from Fort Carlton. In the same year the first survey teams for the Canadian Pacific Railway appeared. In 1876 Lieutenant-Governor Morris arrived at Fort Carlton to conclude Treaty Number 6 with the chiefs of the Cree, the Chipewyan and the Assiniboine. On that day when the Aboriginals surrendered their rights to the prairie lands, the Dumonts acted as interpreters and witnessed the treaty, whose provisions contained the seed of later disputes between the government of Canada and the prairie peoples.

In fact, Treaty Number 6 and the treaty signed the following year with the Blackfoot Confederacy reminded the Métis that, though the Aboriginals were at least assured their reservations, no grants of land had been made to them. As early as 1873, the Métis of Qu'Appelle had petitioned for grants "in compensation of our rights to the lands of the country" and had been ignored by the Dominion government. In 1874 there were similar requests from the Métis of Prince Albert. In his 1876 report, Lieutenant-Governor Morris drew the attention of Alexander Mackenzie's Liberal government to the two urgent questions in the North West: conservation of the buffalo and provision of land for the unsettled Métis, whom he represented as a stabilizing influence on the Aboriginal population.

The conservation of the buffalo gained some attention, and in 1877 the Council of the Northwest Territories passed an ordinance that, if it had been sustained, might have preserved considerable herds for at least a few more years. Wasteful killing was forbidden; calves and cows could only be killed between August and November. But the ordinance was made useless by the very people it was intended to benefit. The Aboriginals objected to any kind of regulation of their hunting because they regarded the buffalo as a gift of Manitou with which the white men had no right to interfere. Dumont and his fellow Métis, though they had introduced their own conservationist measures, objected to the ordinance because it made provisions favouring the Aboriginals and thus depriving the Métis of what they regarded as their equal rights as natives of the prairie. Opposition to the ordinance was so strong that the council repealed it in 1878 and abandoned the buffalo to their fate.

The destruction of the buffalo, now almost complete, made the problem of land on the Saskatchewan even more acute, particularly since the hunters who had once wandered freely into American territory were now being forced back over the border by the U.S. cavalry. Many made their way north to Batoche and St. Laurent where they formed a wild and discontented element in the Métis population.

In addition to these hunters without herds, the settlements of the Saskatchewan also included an influx of more sophisticated Métis from the Red River with their own reasons for discontent. Some of them were farmers who had failed in competition with

Signing the 1876 treaty at Fort Carlton

Storm Clouds on the Saskatchewan

more aggressive Canadian settlers or had been defrauded of lands granted to them in the Manitoba settlement. There were others who had thought themselves men of consequence on the Red River and had tried futilely to collaborate with the new Canadian rulers. These men, like Louis Schmidt, who had been a civil servant, and Charles Nolin, who had been minister of agriculture in an early provincial government, were disillusioned with the settlement in Manitoba and feared that the betrayal would be repeated on the Saskatchewan. They also possessed a political sophistication that would give a sharper direction to the Métis movement.

As early as 1877 Gabriel Dumont re-emerged as leader when the Métis began to present their grievances to the outside authorities. First they asked for help in building a school, which was eventually granted in 1880. Then in 1878, they held a mass meeting, once again outside the church of St. Laurent, in which they framed a petition asking for representation on the Territorial Council (which at this time contained no representative of the Aboriginal peoples), for aid with grain and farm implements like that promised to the Aboriginals under the treaties and, as a matter of particular urgency, "that the Government should cause to be surveyed, with the least possible delay, the lands occupied and cultivated by the half-breeds or old residents of the country, and that patents therefore be granted to them."

This was one of many petitions from Métis in all parts of

the western prairies, but though a Métis member was appointed to the Territorial Council, the land question was shelved first by the Liberal government and then by the Conservatives who returned to power later in 1878. Prime Minister Sir John A. Macdonald was also minister of the interior and directly responsible for dealing with the land claims of the Métis. Instead of immediately solving the problem, so similar to that which had led to the Red River rising of 1869, Macdonald procrastinated. He received repeated warnings. Alexander Morris, as he retired from the lieutenant-governorship of the Territories, remarked,

"It is a crying shame that the half-breeds have been ignored. It will result in trouble and is most unjust." The deputy minister of the interior, Colonel J.S. Dennis, who had actually served against Riel on the Red River, urged immediate action. Archbishop Tache told Macdonald, "Friendly disposed, they (the Métis) will mightily contribute to the maintenance of peace; dissatisfied, they would...render the settlement of the country next thing to impossible."

Macdonald's refusal to act is all the more difficult to understand since no new legislation was needed. Clause 31 of the 1878 Dominion Lands Act gave authority, by order of council, to grant land to "half-breeds resident in the Northwest Territories outside the limits of Manitoba."

But while the authorities in Ottawa procrastinated in settling the Métis claims, they were already sending surveyors into the prairies to divide the land into mile-square sections according to the American survey system. Under the provisions of the new land act, homesteaders—under certain conditions—would be allowed quarter-sections, but present occupiers of the land had no protection under the law, since they were regarded as squatters. The government did nothing to ease the fears of the people who saw the surveyors at work.

Even those Métis—and Gabriel Dumont was among them—who were lucky enough to find their land designated for homesteading were faced with the fact that the surveyors ignored the Métis preference for long, narrow riverfront lots. But the greatest anxiety of all was that while Ottawa procrastinated, every Métis remained legally a squatter. At a time when strangers were rapidly moving into the country, the Métis had no title to their land. These strangers were not only Canadian or British settlers, all of whom shared with the Métis their anxieties over delays in obtaining land titles, but also included the agents of land speculators attempting to secure large tracts at the expense of existing occupants.

As the Métis tried to draw attention to their plight, they were often supported by priests and by members of the local government, and, later on, by Canadian settlers. But the original initiatives came from the Métis of St. Laurent and the vital force in St. Laurent was still Gabriel Dumont.

In 1880 Gabriel led the movement that forced the Territorial Council to withdraw a new toll on wood cut from Crown lands—

the former common lands of the Métis. In June 1881 he organized petitions that asked the Territorial Council to give immediate attention to the Métis demands for land titles. When nothing had happened by the following summer, his mark headed the signatures to another petition, drawn up by Charles Nolin, in which the Métis protested against regulations that required payment for land they had already settled, if it happened to fall into one of the sections not available for homesteading. Asking to be exempted from the homestead regulations and requesting a survey adapted to their traditional way of landholding, the Métis proudly ended this petition:

Charles Nolin

> *Having been so long regarded as the masters of this country, having defended it against the Indians at the cost of our blood, we do not consider that we are asking too much when we call on the government to allow us to occupy our lands in peace and to exempt us from the regulation by making free grants of land to the Métis of the Northwest.*

Even this request, supported by the priests who lived among the Métis, received no reply. The authorities insisted that the surveys must proceed according to the system already laid down; there would be no exceptions. Finally, at the end of 1882, Macdonald acknowledged that a problem existed and proposed to send a special delegate into the West to investigate land claims. But it was not until 1884 that the first representative of the Ottawa government, an inspector of Dominion lands named William Pearce, was sent into the area. But Pearce knew no French and investigated only the claims of those who could speak to him in English. He left the French Métis claims to the bilingual Dominion land agent in Prince Albert, who went to St. Laurent in May 1884. But he in turn waited until October to send his report to Ottawa, where it was mislaid until February 1885. By that time it was too late. The patience of the Métis had run out; they had brought Louis Riel back to Canada to advise and inspire them; and they were already bent on their own course of action.

Chapter 8
The Coming of Louis Riel

In the early summer of 1884 when the Métis delegates came to invite him to the Saskatchewan, Louis Riel was running a school for Métis children at St. Peter's Mission on the Sun River in Montana. The idea of calling on him for advice and perhaps assistance had been discussed for months by the more discontented Métis. Finally it was proposed at a meeting on March 22, 1884 in the house of Abraham Montour in St. Laurent. Some of the leading Métis, including Gabriel Dumont, Charles Nolin and the old merchant Batoche, as well as young militants like Napoleon Nault and Damase Carrière, were there. They came to discuss a proposal by W.H. Jackson, Canadian secretary of the Settlers' Union, urging common action among the French- and English-speaking Métis, and the Canadian settlers.

The men considered collaboration with other discontented groups and discussed new ways to awaken the Canadian government to the realities of the Métis situation. This appears to have been the first occasion on which armed rebellion was discussed, at the initiative not of Gabriel Dumont, who still wished to try peaceful means, but of younger, more impatient men. Napoleon Nault suggested asking Riel's advice. The idea immediately appealed to the assembly, for though he had been driven into exile, Riel was seen as the man, who 15 years before, had forced the Canadian government into an agreement with the Métis. Dumont supported the idea and suggested calling a general assembly of the Saskatchewan Métis.

On April 28 several hundred men gathered in the melting snow outside old Isidore Dumont's log house. After hours of discussion, the meeting passed several resolutions that repeated the demands for land titles, called for a more representative Territorial Council and criticized the government for its neglect of the Aboriginals, who had been driven to the edge of starvation by the extinction of the buffalo herds. The members also

elected a committee of six, including Gabriel Dumont, to draft
a bill of rights to be submitted to a joint meeting of all the discontented groups.

That meeting of Métis, Canadian and British settlers took
place at the Lindsay schoolhouse between Batoche and Prince
Albert on May 6. There was general agreement about the need
to end the procrastinations of the Dominion government, but
less agreement when Riel's name was mentioned. But the elo-
quence of Andrew Spence, leader of the English-speaking Métis,
swayed the white settlers and eventually they all agreed on
their momentous resolution:

We, the French and English natives of the North-west, knowing that
Louis Riel made a bargain with the Government of Canada in 1870,
which said bargain is contained mostly in what is known as the
"Manitoba Act," have thought it advisable that a delegation be sent to
said Louis Riel, and have his assistance to bring all the matters referred

The Coming of Louis Riel

to in the above regulations in a proper shape and form before the Government of Canada, so that our just demands be granted.

The three delegates chosen for the 1100-kilometre journey to Riel's home were all Métis. Gabriel Dumont and Michel Dumas represented the French-speakers and James Isbister, the English-speakers. Moise Ouelette, Gabriel's brother-in-law and a member of the 1873 Métis council in St. Laurent, accompanied the party unofficially. Though they slipped away quietly on May 19, their departure was known to Justice of the Peace Lawrence Clarke, who immediately wired Lieutenant-Governor Dewdney, suggesting that the delegates be shadowed by the mounted police. He also urged that Riel be arrested if he crossed the border. His message was ignored, and Dumont and his companions rode southward without seeing a single police patrol.

With the help of Gabriel's friends among the Blackfoot, they averaged 60 kilometres a day over terrain that was rough and often trackless. It was only south of the border that they encountered difficulties. The Gros Ventre Aboriginals were not one of the groups with whom Dumont had forged an alliance and they demanded tribute. With his customary diplomacy, Gabriel talked them round, and the little caravan travelled on to Fort Benton and then along the Missouri to the Sun River and St. Peter's Mission.

They reached the mission at eight o'clock on the morning of June 4. Riel was in church but they sent for him. When Riel came out, he shook Gabriel Dumont's hand and held it long in his own. "You seem to me a man from far away," he said to Gabriel. "I do not know you, but you seem to know me." "Indeed I do," answered Gabriel, "and you should know me as well. Don't you remember the name of Gabriel Dumont—" "Of course," Riel answered, "I am happy to see you again. But excuse me; I must go back to finish hearing the mass."

Shortly afterwards, when told of the Métis mission, Riel seemed surprised. His reply was extraordinary, emerging from a mind filled with omens and symbols, and Gabriel remembered it ever afterwards. "God wants you to understand that you have taken the right way, for there are four of you and you have arrived on the fourth of June. And you wish to have a fifth to return with you. I cannot give my answer today. Wait until tomorrow morning, and I will have a decision for you."

The next morning Dumont and Dumas accompanied Riel

to the mission church to confess and receive communion. Then they went back to join Isbister and Ouelette at Riel's house, and Dumont asked for a decision. "I gave my heart to my nation 15 years ago," Riel answered, "and I am ready to give it again. But I cannot leave my young family behind. If you can arrange to take us all, I will go with you." "No difficulty," Gabriel answered. "With our three vehicles we have room for you all." Riel required a few days to wind up his employment as teacher, and the delegates agreed to wait. On June 9 Riel taught his last class, and on the next morning Gabriel led the little caravan along the banks of the Sun River.

The journey back to Batoche was uneventful. No police waited at the border, and June passed quietly into July before Dumont and his companions reached the parklands beside the South Saskatchewan. About 25 kilometres from Batoche, at Tourond's Coulee, which the English called Fish Creek, they were met by a cavalcade of 60 Métis horsemen, shouting their welcomes to Riel and firing salutes from their muskets and Winchesters as they sang the proud and violent songs of Pierre Falcon. They escorted the travellers to Tourond's farm, where 50 wagonloads of older people, women and children had gathered around the whitewashed buildings. Riel wept when he saw so many comrades of the Red River days, forced to leave their homes in Manitoba for the far prairies. But there was a moment of tension when he came face-to-face with his cousin Charles Nolin, who had opposed him at Fort Garry in 1869. Gabriel Dumont assured Riel of Nolin's present devotion to the Métis cause, and the old rivals seemed to be reconciled.

After a night at Gabriel's house beside the ferry, the Riels moved into the large house Nolin had built for himself in Batoche. There was a gathering outside the church of Batoche, which was too small to hold all the people who came to welcome the legendary Louis Riel. Aboriginals came as well as English- and French-speaking Métis. Riel told them that—like the Red River settlement—the North West could become a part of the Dominion of Canada only with the free consent of its people, after an agreement had been reached between them and the Canadians negotiating as two equal nations.

Gabriel Dumont never sought glory for its own sake, and during the first four months after Riel's arrival, he was content to play a secondary, though still active, role in Métis affairs.

The Coming of Louis Riel

He submitted the report of the delegation to Montana at a meeting in Batoche on July 8, 1884. Delegates of all the malcontent groups from as far away as Prince Albert and Fort Carlton attended the meeting. Three days later Dumont accompanied Riel to a meeting before a non-Métis audience, again in the Lindsay schoolhouse, where Riel's eloquent moderation won over the Canadian settlers and reassured the anxious priests.

Nevertheless, time and events were playing into the hands of Dumont and the activists. Crops were poor that year in St. Laurent, and Ottawa showed no signs of moving towards a settlement of Métis grievances. The Métis and the Canadian settlers became involved in an apparently endless series of meetings devoted to framing a common petition to the federal government. Still hoping for an alliance of all native peoples, Métis as well as Aboriginals, Dumont influenced Riel to meet with discontented Aboriginal chiefs.

Dumont appeared again as a major force when Bishop Grandin and the lieutenant-governor's secretary, Amadée Forget, visited St. Laurent in September. Riel and his associates were concerned with the aloofness of the Catholic clergy, compared with the support Riel had received from priests on the Red River in 1869–70. In an attempt to involve the Church more deeply, the Métis presented a written address to the bishop as he was about to bless the new bell in the church at Batoche. Grandin agreed to a meeting on September 5 in the church of St. Laurent. He was accompanied by Forget and by Fathers André, Fourmond and Vegreville.

Emerging from his recent silence, Dumont opened the meeting. He spoke simply and with deep emotion, explaining how the deliberate absence of priests from the Métis gatherings caused uneasiness among members of the community. He begged Grandin to explain the attitude of the Church. It was clear that Gabriel had reached a point of inner crisis, where the need for decisive action conflicted with his desire not to break with the priests. Grandin found a later and more intimate conversation with Gabriel even more disturbing: "I fear our poor Métis are making mistakes, and that we shall be blamed for it."

Forget spent the next night at Joseph Vandal's house near Gabriel's Crossing, and Dumont brought him a written version of the demands made the day before at St. Laurent. He went on to describe the feelings of frustration that had led his people to send for Riel. He carefully defined Riel's role: "We need him here as our political leader. In other matters I am the chief here." He emphasized the common interests of Aboriginals and Métis and the bonds uniting them and insisted that the Métis would resist any attempt by the authorities to arrest Riel.

The main result of the meeting between Grandin and the Métis leaders was the creation, under the bishop's patronage, of a religious confraternity, the Union Métisse de Saint-Joseph, inaugurated at St. Laurent on September 24. The priests hoped that the Union would serve as a channel through which the Church's influence might aid the solution of Métis problems. Riel interpreted the Union more politically, and while he acknowledged his loyalty to the Pope and Queen Victoria, he declared that the new organization was a recognition of Métis nationhood.

Lieutenant-Governor Edgar Dewdney

Meanwhile, Sir John A. Macdonald chose this time of tension in the prairies to wire Lieutenant-Governor Dewdney from Ottawa: "I suppose...there will be no trouble until winter sets in and the roads closed (*sic*)," adding, with tired cynicism, that "no amount of concession" would stop people from "grumbling and agitating."

It was in this discouraging atmosphere that, on December 16, the petition of the aggrieved groups in the Saskatchewan country was sent off to the secretary of state in Ottawa, J.A. Chapleau, under cover of a letter signed by W.H. Jackson, the Canadian settlers' leader, and Andrew Spence, the English-speaking Métis secretary of the joint committee. The petition—which we must regard as the basic document of the North West Rebellion that followed it—asked for a responsible provincial government elected by ballot, for representation in Ottawa, for modification of the homestead laws and the granting of land patents to the Métis, for better treatment of the Aboriginals and for a railway to Hudson's Bay and reduced railway tariffs to satisfy the Canadians settlers. Chapleau acknowledged the petition and a copy was sent to the colonial office in London.

In the North West the people waited for a reply, shifting backward and forward from optimism to pessimism, according to their interpretations of the actions of the authorities. Finally, on February 2, 1885, D.H. MacDowall, local member of the Territorial Council, wired Ottawa to say that the Métis showed "great discontent at no reply to representation." On February 4 Macdonald wired Dewdney, saying that the cabinet had decided to "investigate claims of half-breeds." Dewdney transmitted the substance of the wire not to Riel or to Dumont, whom the Métis acknowledged as their local leader, but to Nolin, who had no significant standing among the Saskatchewan Métis.

This telegram, lacking any specific government commitment and communicated through Nolin rather than through the recognized Métis leaders, marked the turning point in events along the Saskatchewan, as winter moved into the spring of 1885. There had always been a group among the Métis who believed that violence was the only way to convince Ottawa of the reality of their grievances. At first Gabriel Dumont, with the deep sense of social responsibility he had shown during the years of the St. Laurent commune, was not among them. But as the petitioning of 1884 brought no better result than Ottawa's vague talk of another investigation, Gabriel's patience ended. He was too realistic to hope that the Métis could win a long war, but he believed that a well-conducted guerrilla campaign might force the Dominion government into genuine negotiations.

The need for rebellion determined the course of events in February and March 1885. When they received Macdonald's telegram, Dumont told Riel that their year of work had been wasted. The government would respond not to petitions, but to drastic action. After reading the telegram, Riel banged the table and shouted, "Within forty days Ottawa shall have my answer." Both he and Dumont knew what the answer would be.

Chapter 9
Provisional Government

On February 24, 1885 Dumont and Riel called a meeting at Batoche to discuss Macdonald's telegram. Fathers Moulin, Fourmond and Vegreville were among those in the church on that momentous day. Inspector Gagnon of the mounted police found it prudent to stay outside.

Riel began with a tirade against the government and its ruthless theft of the West from the Aboriginal peoples. Then he announced quietly that his task was ended. The petition had been sent and an answer received. A commission would consider the Métis grievances; he would return to help his neighbours in Montana. The church erupted in shouts of protest, the loudest coming from Dumont and others who were committed to action. And when Riel, hinting at extreme measures, asked the people if they were willing to accept the consequences of his continuing leadership, they shouted their agreement.

The new strategy began to emerge a week later when Riel stood on the church steps at St. Laurent and said openly that the Métis might have to resort to force. The next day, March 2, he asked Father André's permission to form a provisional government. But since an established Canadian government now existed, Father André refused to give his permission, insisting that it was a different situation from the Red River in 1869. At a joint meeting with the English-speaking malcontents on the next day, Riel and Dumont appeared at the head of a column of 60 armed Métis. Riel claimed the mounted police were trying to arrest him, and pointing at his armed followers, he said, "These are the real police." After this incident the Canadian and British settlers drew away from Riel, and the English-speaking Métis began to assume an attitude of watchful neutrality. The French-speaking Métis were standing alone.

But events had gone beyond the halting point. At a secret meeting on March 5, the leading Métis drew up a document that engaged them "to save our souls by making ourselves live in righteousness night and day in all things and in whatever place we may be" and "to save our country from wicked government by taking up arms whenever it shall be necessary." Led by Dumont and Riel, all 11 men present signed or put their marks to the oath. When Dumont and Riel went to Charles Nolin's house and asked him to add his signature, Nolin was reluctant to commit himself. He suggested that if the Métis leaders seriously desired to work for the glory of God, they might hold a novena—nine days of public prayers and confessions—in the hope that the Holy Spirit might illumine their consciences.

Riel and Dumont agreed; it was a good way to assemble their followers. The novena was to begin on March 10. The priests thought they had won time, but the mounted police were less optimistic. Their spies told them that Dumont was talking of capturing Fort Carlton and that his men were arming for battle. Telegrams sped between the West and Ottawa. On March 18 Commissioner Irvine set off from Regina in the direction of Prince Albert with 100 mounted police, and the *Saskatchewan Herald* reported from Battleford, "Incipient rebellion. Riel and his friends are on the move, and so are the police."

Lawrence Clarke

By the time Irvine set off, Dumont was riding over the countryside gathering followers. He visited all the local Métis communities, and the Cree chiefs Beardy and One Arrow pledged their support. On March 18 Lawrence Clarke arrived at the Batoche ferry on his way back to Fort Carlton. He asked if the Métis were still holding meetings and was told that there were meetings almost every day. "Fine! Fine!" shouted Clarke. "But it won't go on much longer. The police are on their way...Tomorrow or the day after they will pick up Riel and Dumont."

When they heard this news, Gabriel and Riel rode with 70 armed men into Batoche, where they took arms and ammunition from John Kerr's store and captured Kerr and two non-Métis customers as hostages.

From Kerr's store the rebels rode on to the church in Batoche. When Father Moulin protested, Riel jeered, "The priest is a Protestant," and shouted, "Rome is fallen," as he led his followers inside the church and promised that a provisional government would be established. At a mass meeting on the following day,

March 19. Riel nominated Dumont as "Adjutant General of the Métis nation...at the head of the army." He was elected by acclamation. Dumont then proceeded to pick the 12 councillors, also elected without question. Riel refused any official position, and the only non-Métis member of the "Provisional Government of the Saskatchewan" was William Henry Jackson, chosen as secretary.

Dumont immediately organized his small army of 300 men according to the traditions of the buffalo hunt. Two captains of scouts were picked, each with 10 men, to patrol the east and west shores of the river; the rest of the men were divided into 10 fighting companies each with a captain to lead it. Dumont proposed that the Aboriginals should immediately be invited to join the rebellion. There should be surprise assaults on Fort Carlton and Prince Albert to seize arms and ammunition and to gain a tactical advantage by striking the first blow. Riel and Dumont ended in council, with a resolution that Fort Carlton should be taken if possible without bloodshed, but that "in the event of our being forced to fight, justice will compel us to resort to arms."

Fort Carlton

A mounted police detachment located at Fort Carlton was in the charge of Leif Crozier, whom Dumont had confronted at St. Laurent 10 years before. The provisional government sent Crozier an ultimatum demanding surrender: "You will be required to give up completely the situation which the Canadian Government has placed you in, at Carlton and Battleford, together with all government properties."

Crozier did not surrender, and the Métis did not attack Fort Carlton on March 23, the day their ultimatum specified. On March 24 the English-speaking Métis decided to send yet another petition and to remain neutral in any fighting that might follow. Dumont's Métis were left to face their first battle alone. It was a battle which Riel had not foreseen and which Dumont had to fight.

Chapter 10
Blood at Duck Lake

The fighting started on March 26. Dumont learned that Crozier's spies were in the area of Duck Lake, on the opposite bank of the river from Batoche, and he decided to take men to pillage weapons and supplies from the stores in Duck Lake before the mounted police cut them off. The mission was successful, and during the night Dumont captured two of Crozier's scouts. Then, as dawn was breaking, the shout went up, "The police are coming!" Warned that the Métis were likely to occupy Duck Lake but unaware that they had already done so, Crozier had sent a detachment of 15 police and seven Prince Albert volunteers, under Sergeant Stewart and his guide Thomas McKay, to fetch government provisions that had been left in one of the stores.

Dumont and his 30 men immediately set off and intercepted the police party. A noisy verbal battle followed, and a couple of guns went off accidentally, but little harm was done. With the police obviously outnumbered, Sergeant Stewart quickly decided it was no time for valour. He and his party turned their sleighs and hurried back to Fort Carlton, while Dumont and his men returned jubilantly to Duck Lake.

But, as Dumont relayed in the narrative of the North West Rebellion that he dictated years afterwards, "We had hardly let our horses out to feed than we again heard someone shouting, 'The police are coming!'" In Fort Carlton, the disgrace of Stewart's retreat had been felt deeply by Crozier and his officers, who feared that if they did not redeem the situation the rebellion would spread quickly. Crozier might have waited until Commissioner Irvine arrived with his police reinforcements, but the Prince Albert volunteers were eager for action, and Crozier decided to move immediately and to lead the entire garrison of Fort Carlton in an immediate assault on Duck Lake.

Crozier's force consisted of 56 mounted police and 43 Prince Albert volunteers. Some were mounted; some rode on sleighs. They took a seven-pound [three-kilogram] cannon. Meanwhile, the news of the first encounter had brought 300 Métis riding in from Batoche and St. Laurent. Riel was with them, as well as some Cree from the nearby reserves. Dumont immediately set off with an advance party to establish an ambush. He chose a spot with plenty of low bush, a gully where his men could creep unseen, and to one side a log house where sharp-shooters could hide. But Crozier's scouts detected the ambush, and he ordered his men to halt, form their 20 sleighs into a barricade and prepare the cannon for battle.

Meanwhile, Gabriel's brother Isidore and an elderly Aboriginal named Aseeweyin had ridden forward to parley. McKay, the interpreter, came up to them, with Crozier close behind. Aseeweyin apparently reached for the interpreter's gun and as McKay fired at him, Crozier gave the order for a general volley. Isidore Dumont fell dead from his horse. Gabriel, enraged at his brother's death, ordered his men to shoot back. A merciless fire was directed on the police and volunteers from three sides of the ambush, while Riel waved a cross he had taken from a chapel near Duck Lake and shouted, "In the name of God who created us, answer their fire!"

In his excitement, the police gunner put the shot in before the charge and the cannon stopped firing. Gabriel Dumont

The fight at Duck Lake

Sir John A. Macdonald

received a scalp wound, and his younger brother Edouard took over the Métis command. But Dumont's tactics had forced Crozier's men to choose between flight or extermination, and soon the superintendent gave the order for retreat. Ten of his men had been killed and 13 wounded, two fatally; the Métis had lost five men killed and three wounded, including Dumont. It was a Métis victory, and the Dumonts wanted to pursue and slaughter the fleeing enemy, but Riel begged them "for the love of God, to kill no more of them," saying that, "enough blood had already been shed."

Crozier returned in confusion to Fort Carlton, where he found Commissioner Irvine waiting with a force of 108 men, which might have been enough to turn defeat into victory at Duck Lake. Irvine reproached Crozier for his impetuosity and tried to decide what to do about his indefensible position. The police were cooped up with more than 200 people, including women and children from the neighbouring farms, in a broken-down fort at the foot of hills on which Métis scouts were already establishing themselves. Irvine expected that the Métis would attack either Fort Carlton or Prince Albert, which was virtually without defenders. He decided to march to Prince Albert, which could be fortified and where there were people who needed protection. He was helped by Riel's piety, which required that the Métis devote the whole day after the battle to prayers for the souls of their dead.

Irvine and his men spent March 27 loading stores at Fort Carlton for evacuation on the following day. But that night a fire broke out in the fort, and the garrison departed in the pre-dawn darkness, anxious to flee from the revealing flames. As soon as Dumont's scouts told him the first wagons were leaving Fort Carlton, he wanted to attack them in a large spruce wood through which they would have to pass. "We could have killed a lot of them," he remarked, "but Riel, who kept us always on the leash, was opposed to the project." Once again, Riel's dream of a treaty without bloodshed gave the enemy breathing space. Dumont, who recognized the strategic advantages they were throwing away, raged inwardly while he did his best to calm the restlessness of his young captains. They had to be content with the empty victory of riding and taking formal possession of Fort Carlton.

Far off in Ottawa, the news of Duck Lake finally spurred Sir John A. Macdonald into action. On March 26, the very day of the Duck Lake fight, Macdonald stood in the House of Commons and declared—in the face of seven years of warnings from every side—"We are quite unaware of the approximate cause of the half-breed rising under Riel." Yet in fact he had been making military preparations for some time. Three days before Duck Lake he had instructed Major-General Frederick Dobson Middleton, commander of the Canadian militia, to proceed to Winnipeg. Middleton arrived on March 27 and immediately continued westward with a hastily mobilized local militiamen regiment, the 90th Rifles. At Qu'Appelle they set up a base for the militiamen who were being mobilized in Ontario, Quebec and Manitoba.

Major-General Frederick D. Middleton (centre, on white horse). Leif Crozier is at the back, left (arrow) in white helmet.

Chapter 11
Victory at Fish Creek

Big Bear (top) and Poundmaker (bottom left) joined Dumont's rebellion. Sitting Bull (bottom right) did not.

Dumont had expected that the rebellion would spread over the prairies, but his dream was only partially realized. The Cree and a few Assiniboine rose on the North Saskatchewan under the rebel chiefs Poundmaker and Big Bear. But the Blackfoot Confederacy remained aloof, and only a few of the Sioux remembered their old alliance with the Dumonts and rode to join the rebels at Batoche. The most powerful prairie chiefs, Crowfoot, Piapot and Sitting Bull, ignored Dumont's appeals, and even among the Métis none of the other large settlements in the prairies joined Batoche in armed resistance.

Dumont's own plans for action in the weeks after Duck Lake and before Middleton's army could assemble and march to Batoche were based largely on the need to convert the uncommitted Aboriginals and Métis. Middleton had gathered 6,000 men. Many of these would be needed to keep open the long routes of communication from Winnipeg and to defend the depots at Qu'Appelle and Swift Current. By the time columns were sent to deal with Poundmaker and Big Bear, there were between 800 and 1,000 men available to march north to Batoche, accompanied by artillery and Lieutenant Howard's famous Gatling gun. Middleton started from Qu'Appelle on April 6 and proceeded slowly, since he still expected troops and supplies. He reached Clarke's Crossing, about 60 kilometres south of Batoche, on April 17. While waiting for reinforcements there, he divided his column into two parts to advance up both sides of the Saskatchewan.

Dumont was informed of everything Middleton did, for he had scouts operating as far south as Qu'Appelle, and one of his spies, Jérome Henry, was a teamster in the Canadian column. On the basis of their information, he worked out a strategy of guerrilla harassment. He wanted to send men into the southeast to blow up railway tracks and destroy bridges so that Middleton would be cut off from his bases in eastern Canada. According to Dumont, he also "proposed we go ahead of the troops, harass them by night, and above all prevent them from sleeping, believing this was a good way to demoralize them and make them lose heart." If the disruptive

The Gatling gun

tactics had been successful in hampering and perhaps halting the advance of the Canadian columns, the uncommitted Aboriginals and Métis might have committed themselves on the rebel side.

But once again Riel opposed Dumont. He argued that the mounted police occupied Prince Albert in strength and that with only 350 fighting men equipped and a mere 200 effective rifles, the Métis could not spare men to harass Middleton. He told Dumont that guerrilla tactics were too much like Aboriginal warfare and that night attacks might involve firing on French Canadians who had joined Middleton's column. Dumont protested that, French or English, he could hardly regard them as friends if they came to fight against him. But Riel replied, "If you knew them you would not want to deal with them in that way."

Perhaps Riel was swayed as much by visionary inspiration as by earthly reasoning, for his dream of creating a new order in the prairies occupied much of his time and attention during the brief weeks between the Duck Lake battle and the arrival of Middleton's army. If God were to intervene miraculously on the side of the Métis, his will must be obeyed beforehand. The council had to enter into theological questions, passing resolutions that an all-merciful God could not possibly have decreed a never-ending hell and that the Sabbath should be observed, as Genesis decreed, on Saturday. When the priests protested against such innovations, Riel declared that papal infallibility had come to an end and that he had been delegated by the Holy Spirit to reform the Church. He favoured waiting on Divine Providence in dealing with the enemies of the Métis. Let the soldiers come when they pleased, and God would give the sign to strike.

Despite his shrewd military judgment of the situation, Dumont accepted Riel's decisions, though why he should have done so—given his influence as a leader of the Saskatchewan Métis—seems somewhat mysterious. His own explanation is much less simple than it first appears. "I yielded to Riel's judgment," he said, "although I was convinced that, from a humane standpoint, mine was the better plan; but I had confidence in his faith and his prayers, and that God would listen to him."

There was an obvious division within Dumont. On one hand was the highly practical hunter and warrior who never really abandoned his view of the strategy needed for the rebellion. On the other hand was the pious Métis in whose eyes Riel had replaced the missionaries who had lost credit by refusing to support the rebellion. The balance between these opposing views was tipped partly by Dumont's loyalty to Riel and partly by a bond of affection that had sprung up between the men during the months since they had ridden together from Montana. Whatever the reason, Dumont accepted Riel's ban on action until the eleventh hour, and there is no doubt that the indecision that marked the early days of the rebellion isolated the Métis of Batoche and prevented their struggles from spreading over the prairies.

It might well have been otherwise. Sandford Fleming, the engineer in charge of the surveys for the Canadian Pacific Railway, warned Macdonald, "Even a momentary check at the crisis would cause thousands of Indians who are at present quiet to rise." Dumont was militarily and politically a wiser man than the Riel he had called in to solve his people's problems. But Gabriel's advice was not heeded until Middleton began to move north on the last lap of his journey to Batoche, and by that time the moment for a general uprising in the prairies had passed.

By the time the Canadian army lurched forward from Clarke's Crossing on April 23, Dumont and his captains had lost their patience. Dumont could no longer endure letting Middleton "move around as he wanted" in his beloved Saskatchewan country. "I told Riel...that I intended to go out and shoot at the invaders, and that my men supported me."

Riel at last gave in, and Dumont immediately sent messengers to Poundmaker and Big Bear, telling them of the coming struggle and asking them to lead their warriors to the defence of Batoche. His scouts told him that Middleton's column was camped 10 kilometres south of Fish Creek, and he proposed to make a night attack, with sentries silently stabbed, the prairie set on fire and 200 Métis horsemen sweeping through the camp to kill, burn, plunder and then vanish into the dark. But that night Middleton's scouts rode out to collect a store of forage they had seen during the day, and Dumont's scouts wrongly concluded that the Canadians were on their guard. The night attack never took place.

Having lost his advantage, Dumont decided on a daylight ambush at Tourond's Coulee, where Fish Creek ran down to join the South Saskatchewan. Through the coulee and up onto the parkland south of Batoche wound the trail which—as Jérome Henry had informed Dumont—Middleton and his column intended to take. It was a natural trap. Marksmen carefully placed in the creek bed and on the slopes above could command the road all through the ravine, and low, thick woods came down on the edge of the creek at the bridge that Middleton's men would have to cross.

Accompanied by Riel, Dumont set off at nightfall with a motley column of about 200 Métis and Aboriginals, some mounted and some on foot. Thirty men had been left at Batoche under the command of Edouard Dumont. At midnight, after halting several times on Riel's insistence to say the rosary, the column stopped to kill and roast a couple of cows for supper. Here they were overtaken by messengers saying that the mounted police were coming by the Qu'Appelle road to surprise Batoche; reinforcements were needed. Riel returned with 50 men, and Dumont rode on with the rest to attack a Canadian force more than five times as large. At seven o'clock, as he and

Fish Creek Battle

his men were breakfasting on another slaughtered beast, a scout warned him that Middleton's forces were nearing the coulee.

"I therefore placed a hundred and thirty of our men in a hollow on the left bank of Fish Creek, opposite Tourond's house," Gabriel recollected, "and hid their horses in the woods. I went on with twenty horsemen to take cover along the path that the troops would follow. I did not intend to charge them until the others thrust them back, and I gave my main force instructions not to attack them until they were all in the coulee."

Despite Dumont's precautions, his men disobeyed his orders and rode across the track leading from Clarke's Crossing to Gabriel's Crossing. Middleton's scouts saw their tracks and alerted the army. Dumont's own foolhardiness spoiled his remaining chance of taking the enemy by surprise. He started to chase a Canadian scout. "I...was about to overtake him, when somebody fired at me. My people shouted to me that I was riding into a troop of forty men whom I had not seen, so intent was I on catching my prey."

The battle had started, and Dumont's carefully laid plans had been frustrated. His group of 20 marksmen was now opposing Middleton's entire force. After firing from the cover of the bushes in the face of the fierce enemy attack, Dumont galloped off with his men to join the party he had left higher up the ravine. He found his troops deserting in panic at the sight of Middleton's artillery, which had not yet come into action. Even when Dumont stopped 15 men who were about to desert, only 47 of the original 130 were left. With the 15 men who remained of his own troop, he now had fewer than 60 men to resist 400 riflemen trying to shoot their way through the ravine.

But Dumont had no intention of giving up. He was not in good shape; his head wound from Duck Lake had received no medical attention and was painful and inflamed. But he was so excited that he seemed unaware of his discomfort and was able to inspire the men who had chosen to stay. They were the pick of his people, companions from the days of the buffalo hunt and the best of the young men.

All day, as they lay in their shallow rifle pits on the edge of the woodland, Gabriel and his men hoped for help from Batoche. But Riel, who prayed for hours on end with his arms held up in the shape of a cross and exhorted the women and children to do likewise, would not send any men, even though the police attack from Qu'Appelle had not materialized. Finally, Edouard Dumont's patience ended. "My brothers are there," he said, "and I will not let them be killed without going to their aid." He gathered 80 horsemen, Métis and Aboriginals, and rode hard to Fish Creek. At nightfall he led his cavalry in a shooting charge into the coulee. They forced the Canadians back and Middleton withdrew his troops. Edouard arrived none too soon; the Métis were running out of ammunition and from noon onwards had been firing infrequently, but accurately.

It was a victory for Dumont. He and his men had held back and severely mauled a much larger army. Even his enemies were full of admiration. Middleton admitted in a wire to Ottawa, "Their plans were well arranged beforehand and had my scouts not been well to the front we should have been attacked in the ravine and probably wiped out." The *Toronto Mail* appeared on the day after the battle with a report that "Gabriel Dumont commands the rebels, and does it with consummate skill." But, like Duck Lake, it was not a decisive victory. As far as the Canadians were concerned, it was an annoying delay in the eventual suppression of the rebellion, since Middleton had to rest his men and reorganize his column. But it was not the kind of disastrous route that might influence Macdonald to change his policy and start negotiations.

Chapter 12
The Fall of Batoche

After the battle, Middleton waited at Fish Creek for reinforcements. The column marching up the west side of the river was ferried across to strengthen the main column, but Middleton still awaited other men coming from Swift Current on the commandeered Hudson's Bay Company sternwheeler, the *Northcote*. The *Northcote* did not leave Swift Current until April 23, and it took 14 days making its way laboriously down the sandbank-obstructed river to Clarke's Crossing.

At last, on May 7, the Canadian column was on the move again—850 men with four cannon, Lieutenant Howard's Gatling gun and an unwieldy baggage train of 150 wagons, whose beasts ate half the freight they carried. Middleton, who feared more ambushes, had decided to advance along the river trail only as far as Gabriel's Crossing. Then he would strike inland over the open parkland, advancing on Batoche from the east across the stretch of grassland that the Métis called La Belle Prairie. On a small scale, Middleton intended to combine naval and land operations. He had placed 30 soldiers and two officers on the *Northcote*, instructing them to create a diversion by sailing downriver and making a landing below Batoche while the major attack began from the other side.

In Batoche, once again, there was disagreement between Riel and Dumont. Dumont wanted to harass the enemy camps and to ambush the Canadians in the woods along their way. Riel answered that God had told him in visions to wait until Batoche was attacked and then defend it. But the Métis were not suited for siege warfare against even an amateur army like Middleton's. Their strength lay in their knowledge of the open prairies, where, under men like Gabriel Dumont and his brothers, they might have kept the Canadian forces skirmishing in constant tension for months, perhaps for years.

Dumont and his best captains knew this, but when Riel would not be moved by their arguments, they allowed their strange respect for this mystical leader to overcome their common sense. They began building their carefully spaced rifle pits and trenches, disguised by loopholed logs and parapets of turf. These would make the defenders of Batoche invisible and invincible as long as their ammunition lasted. But they lacked both arms and ammunition. A few, like Gabriel, owned Winchesters and fair supplies of cartridges; others, like Edouard Dumont, had captured carbines from Middleton's men; but many had only the most primitive of trade muskets or no firearms at all. They melted the lead linings of tea chests into bullets and cut scrap metal into slugs to be used in shotguns when the buckshot gave out.

Manpower was almost as scarce as lead. Against Middleton's 850 men, Dumont had fewer than 300. Sixty were guarding the west bank of the Saskatchewan; a small party guarded Batoche's Ferry. About 200 were left to man the rifle pits and defend the cluster of shacks and the few large houses that constituted the Métis capital. It is hard to say how high morale was in Batoche. There would be suicidal acts of heroism,

The final assault on Batoche

especially among the older men fighting for a vanishing past. Louis Schmidt, a friend of Riel who did not take part in the battle, estimated that only one-third to one-quarter of the people of Batoche were really committed to resistance.

Certainly their hope of help from the Aboriginals and the other Métis proved futile. Dumont sent an urgent message to Poundmaker, asking for immediate help, but the Aboriginal chief, who had just defeated a Canadian force at Cut Knife Hill, did not start to march towards Batoche until it had fallen. A column of 100 Métis from Lac Ste Anne near Edmonton and a column of 60 Métis from the Battleford region also started off but turned back when messengers brought the news of defeat. Together, these forces might have prevented that defeat.

On May 7, Middleton marched to Gabriel's Crossing where his men burned Dumont's house and pulled down his stables, using the timbers to fortify the upper deck of the *Northcote*. Gabriel's possessions, including his treasured billiard table, were looted. On May 8, Middleton marched east from Gabriel's Crossing and then north, camping beside the trail from Batoche to Humboldt. His plan was that on the next morning the *Northcote* and one column would make their attacks from opposite sides of the village at exactly nine o'clock. But the column moved more slowly than had been planned, while the boat swung round the great bend below the church of Batoche an hour early and started its own battle with the sharpshooters Dumont had placed on either side of the river.

While Dumont's attention was diverted by the *Northcote*, Middleton advanced towards Batoche. But instead of attacking from the east, he turned his army south and established his headquarters in an outlying farm. Then the Canadian soldiers advanced in skirmishing order, and the cannon were established on a knoll about one and a half kilometres from the village. The battle began with bugle calls and with Lieutenant Howard firing a burst or two from his Gatling. The shots went over the heads of the Métis, who were hidden in their rifle pits on the slope of the hill so that they could fire with deadly accuracy at the Canadian riflemen who appeared above them on the skyline.

Dumont settled himself "forward on the prairie, seated on one of my heels, with a knee on the ground," where he could quickly give orders that were shouted from pit to pit. His men never felt he was asking them to do anything he was unwilling to do himself, and his enemies, in their admiring reports to Ottawa, talked of him "fighting all day like a tiger." He carefully supervised the Métis operations—their rushes to outflank the enemy, their feints to give the impression of numbers and their withdrawals into screens of bush or lines of invisible gun pits. Again, their casualties were slight compared with those of the Canadian militiamen. Middleton's cannon pounded away, knocking down and setting fire to buildings in Batoche and on the far side of the river, but doing little harm to the simple Métis fortifications.

The fight on the first day was completely indecisive. Middleton retreated to the protected enclosure he had made at Caron's farm, where his men were kept awake by shots and war cries from Dumont's scouts hovering around the camp. The next two days passed in much the same way, with Middleton's men marching onto the hillside where Métis fire held their attack all day until the bugles sounded and they returned to camp.

The human casualties were almost entirely among the Canadians but the Métis were suffering losses of another kind. By the third night their ammunition was almost exhausted; slugs of metal, nails and even stones were taking the place of bullets.

On the fourth day, May 12, the battle came to an abrupt and unexpected end. During the afternoon Middleton was attempting one of his cautious diversionary manoeuvres, which always failed because the Métis had time to anticipate them. Suddenly, the militia's patience broke. Led by a number of officers disobeying the general's orders, they charged wildly down the hillside and flushed the exhausted Métis out of the rifle pits. There was no real resistance until the defenders made a stand among the houses of the village. It was in this last resistance that most of the Métis deaths took place, including those of valiant patriarchs like Joseph Ouelette, aged 93, and Joseph Vandal, aged 75.

During those final hours in Batoche, Dumont was at his most active.

When the troops entered Batoche...our men first withdrew half a mile. I myself stayed on the higher ground with six of my brave comrades. I held up the enemy's progress there for a whole hour...Then I went down to the riverside, where I ran into seven or eight men who, like plenty of others, were in flight. I asked them to come with me so that we could ambush the enemy. When they refused, I threatened to kill the first

The Fall of Batoche

man who made off. They then came with me, and we kept the English at bay for another half hour.

By now the Métis not already killed or taken prisoner had been pushed out of the village, and in a wood on the outskirts Dumont saw Riel for the last time. Having so often restrained willing fighters, he was now urging unwilling men to continue a lost battle.

"'What are we going to do?' he said as soon as he saw me. 'We are defeated,' I said to him. 'We shall perish. But you must have known, when we took up arms, that we would be beaten. So, they will destroy us.'

"I then told Riel that I must go to our camp to find some blankets. He said I was exposing myself too much, and I answered that the enemy would not be able to kill me. At that moment I felt afraid of nothing."

The siege of Batoche was ended. The Canadians, who had lost all the previous battles, won the war. The Métis cause and the Métis nation as they had existed for almost a century on the prairies had come to an end. Dumont spent the days after the defeat as a fugitive around Batoche, trying to provide for the safety of his wife Madeleine and to arrange for Riel's escape to Montana. During the siege, Madeleine had tended the rebel wounded, and now, with the wives of other men who had defended the village, she was hiding in the woods north of Batoche's ferry. Dumont found her there after he left Riel. He crept back into the occupied village to get blankets for Madeleine and Riel's wife. "The next day I hid my wife farther off, and I went back to the river to see if I could find Riel."

While Dumont was trying to find Riel, the police were trying to find Dumont, and the army reports and telegrams for the first days after the fall of Batoche are full of accounts of his having been sighted at various places in a wide radius around the village. But Gabriel watched his pursuers more carefully than they watched him and always escaped. On the third day, when he realized that he could not live indefinitely around Batoche, Gabriel sent Madeleine to stay with his father, old Isidore,

A group of Métis taken prisoner at Batoche

The Fall of Batoche

who had taken no part in the rising. He then resumed the search for Riel and visited the battlefield to pick up cartridges dropped by the Canadian soldiers.

After dark he went to old Isidore's house and told him that he meant to stay in the region and spend the summer harrying the police with the help of any Métis or Aboriginals who would join him in guerrilla warfare. Isidore urged him to abandon the plan. "I am proud you have not given up," he said, "but if you stay here just to kill people, you will merely be thought an idiot." Isidore advised him to ride for the border and Madeleine added her pleas. Gabriel agreed, but first he wanted to find out what had happened to Riel. The next day, May 15, he learned that Riel had surrendered to Middleton.

Since there was nothing more he could do for Riel or for any of the other Métis, Dumont decided it was time to save himself. He spent the night encamped in a wood with his cousin Jean and Jean's son, young Alexis. Since the way to his father's house was being watched and it was unsafe for Gabriel to go there, he sent Alexis with a message to Madeleine that he was leaving at last and a request for his father to send him some food for the journey. All Isidore could send were six galettes, a kind of bannock made by the Métis, each weighing less than half a kilogram. Gabriel had his own horse, "the best courser in Batoche," his favourite rifle with 90 cartridges and a revolver with 40 rounds, so he felt he could fight off any pursuer. At the edge of the wood, he said goodbye and rode off, but he had hardly ridden a hundred metres when he heard someone shout his name. He turned with his rifle ready, but it was Michel Dumas, who had been with him when he brought Riel from Montana. Dumas had lost his gun and all he had was a few more galettes. "We set out by the Grace of God!" said Dumont, and with those words he ended his account of the rebellion.

Helped on their way by the Aboriginals and Métis they encountered, the two fugitives travelled for 11 days, mostly after dark, before they reached the border. If any police ever saw them, they did not interfere. "I felt I was protected," Gabriel later said. "And I never failed to say to the Holy Virgin: 'You are my mother! Guide me!'" When they were safely across the border, he and Dumas knelt to say the rosary in thankfulness.

Chapter 13
The Long Way Home

In American territory, the two fugitives were arrested by a cavalry patrol and taken to Fort Assiniboine, where they were kept while their case was considered by President Grover Cleveland. After a few days, they were released and began to live as refugees. Gabriel's first concern was to help Riel. He travelled among the Métis communities of Montana and even slipped over the border to organize a rescue plan that the mounted police evidently took quite seriously, for the Regina barracks was guarded by no less than 300 heavily armed men when Riel was hanged on November 15, 1885.

While Gabriel worked to rescue Riel, Madeleine joined him, bringing news that his father Isidore had died. She herself died in the spring of 1886. Now there seemed no reason why Gabriel should not accept the persistent offers that had been made to him ever since he arrived in the United States by Major John Burke, who represented Colonel "Buffalo Bill" Cody. On July 7, 1886 Dumont travelled—his first journey by railway—to Philadelphia and joined the Wild West Show. He was billed as a leader of the North West Rebellion and showed off his marksmanship by riding furiously across the arena and shooting down blue glass balls that a cowboy threw into the air. For a few weeks, while Riel's trial and execution held the news, he was a favourite with American audiences, but the novelty soon wore off. Later in 1886, when the Canadian government issued an amnesty for those who had taken part in the rebellion, Gabriel left the show. But suspicious of the amnesty offer, he did not return to Canada until 1888. For a time he was patronized by the Quebec nationalists and even made a trip to Paris. But he was unhappy among city men and wandered for years in the border regions of Canada and the United States until finally, in 1893, he went home to Batoche.

Here he had kept his old land, but the ferry was in other

hands. He did not attempt to rebuild the house where he and Madeleine had lived, nor did he marry again. Instead he built a little log cabin on the land of young Alexis Dumont, who had now become a farmer at Bellevue, about nine kilometres north of Batoche. Gabriel described himself in official documents at this time as "Voyageur now, Farmer before." He let others use his land and occupied himself mainly with hunting, fishing and a little trading, often being away for weeks on end in the forests and hills. He lived largely in the past, talking often of the rebellion and of the great buffalo hunts.

In the spring of 1906 he went on a hunting trip to Basin Lake in the hills a few kilometres east of Batoche. When he came back, he complained of pains in his chest, but since he seemed in perfect health he decided he had merely strained his muscles. For the next few days he went on in his usual way, walking, fishing and talking to the friends he met by the roadside. On Saturday, May 19, 1906 he again went for a walk. On his return he went to Alexis's house and asked for a bowl of soup. He sat down, ate a few mouthfuls and then, without a word, walked across to a bed and crumpled onto it. His death was immediate.

Gabriel Dumont as he appeared in Buffalo Bill's Wild West Show

When Gabriel Dumont died, the world did not think of him because the world did not know. The cause he fought for so fearlessly, the way of life he personified so vividly had faded out of the national memory; only the local newspapers in Battleford and Prince Albert noticed his passing. But when he was buried in the cemetery at the top of the hill in Batoche, where the dead men of the rebellion lay under their great stark cross, the Métis came riding in from all the settlements in the region, and the Cree tramped from Beardy's and One Arrow's reservations to crowd into the little church scarred with the bullets of Lieutenant Howard's Gatling gun.

Father Moulin, another survivor from the days of the rebellion, conducted the burial service, and the young men of the Dumont clan carried Gabriel to his grave. It overlooked the point on the river where, 21 years earlier, the *Northcote* had come whistling frantically round the bend in the Saskatchewan to open the battle that had marked Gabriel's most heroic hour and the death of the Métis nation.

Gabriel Dumont

1837	Born at St. Boniface
	Leads nomadic life with parents, following the buffalo hunt
1851	Fights in the battle of Grand Coteau
1858	Marries Madeleine Wilkie
1863	Becomes head of the Saskatchewan hunt
1870	Meets Louis Riel at Fort Garry
1872	Establishes ferry service at Gabriel's Crossing
1873	Presides over mass meeting to create Métis constitution
	Named president of community of St. Laurent
1875	St. Laurent council passes new hunt laws to protect buffalo herds
1881	Organizes petitions to Territorial Council demanding land titles for Métis
1884	Travels to Montana to invite Riel to Saskatchewan to help settle Métis grievances
1885	Acclaimed Adjutant General of the Métis nation and head of the army
	His brother Isidore is killed in the fight at Duck Lake
	Battle of Fish Creek
	Métis are defeated at Batoche
1886	Madeleine Dumont dies
	Dumont joins "Buffalo Bill" Cody's Wild West Show
1888	Returns to Canada
1893	Returns to Batoche
1906	Dies on May 19

Further Reading

Bowsfield, Hartwell. *Louis Riel: The Rebel and the Hero*. Toronto: Oxford University Press, 1971.

Dumont, Gabriel. *Gabriel Dumont Speaks*, tr. Michael Barnholden. Vancouver: Talonbooks, 1993.

Howard, Joseph K. *Strange Empire: Louis Riel and the Métis People*. Toronto: James Lewis and Samuel, 1994.

Mika, Nick and Helma. *The Riel Rebellion, 1885*. Belleville, Ont.: Mika Silk Screening, 1972

Morton, Desmond. *The Last War Drum*. Toronto: Hakkert, 1972.

Neering, Rosemary. *Louis Riel*. Markham, Ont.: Fitzhenry & Whiteside, 1999.

Stanley, George F.G. *The Birth of Western Canada*. Toronto: University of Toronto Press, 1992.

_____. *Louis Riel*. Toronto: Ryerson Press, 1963.

Waite, Peter. *John A. Macdonald*, Don Mills, Ont.: Fitzhenry & Whiteside, 1999.

Woodcock, George. *Gabriel Dumont*. Edmonton: Hurtig, 1975. This full-length biography is an excellent source for those wishing to pursue further the subjects and issues raised in this book.

Credits

Index